Copyright © 2023 by Herman Strange (Author)

All rights reserved. This book or any portion thereof may not be reproduced or used in any manner whatsoever without the express written permission of the publisher except for the use of brief quotations in a book review.

This book is copyright protected. This is only for personal use. You cannot amend, distributor, sell, use, quote or paraphrase any part or the content within this book without the consent of the author. Please note the information contained within this document is for educational and entertainment purposes only. Every attempt has been made to provide accurate, up to date and reliable complete information. No warranties of any kind are expressed or implied.

Readers acknowledge that the author is not engaging in the rendering of legal, financial, medical or professional advice. The content of this book has been derived from various sources. Please consult a licensed professional before attempting any techniques outlined in this book.

By reading this document, the readers agree that under no circumstances are the author responsible for any losses, direct or indirect, which are incurred as a result of the use of information contained within this document, including but not limited to errors, omissions or inaccuracies.

Thank you very much for reading this book.

Title: Avoiding for Health-Strategies to Live a Clean and Healthy Lifestyle
Subtitle: A Guide to Reducing Your Exposure to Harmful Substances

Series: Healthy Habits for Life: Building Sustainable Habits for Optimal Health and Wellness
Author: Serenity Tanner

Table of Contents

Introduction **5**
Importance of Avoiding Harmful Substances *6*
Purpose of the Book *8*
Overview of Toxins and How They Affect Health *10*

Chapter 1: Common Toxins and Their Effects **13**
List and Description of Common Toxins *13*
Health Effects of Exposure *17*
Sources of Exposure *21*

Chapter 2: Tracking Your Exposure **24**
Methods for Tracking Exposure *24*
Pros and Cons *27*
Popular Brands and Devices *30*

Chapter 3: Reducing Your Exposure **35**
Methods for Reducing Exposure *35*
Pros and Cons *41*
Popular Brands and Devices *44*

Chapter 4: Toxin-Free Living **46**
Tips and Tricks for Living a Toxin-Free Life *46*
Alternative Products and Services *48*
DIY and Homemade Solutions *50*

Chapter 5: Technology for Toxin-Free Living **53**
Latest Technology for Living a Toxin-Free Life *53*
Pros and Cons *56*

Popular Brands and Devices *58*
Chapter 6: Comparing and Contrasting Methods .. 63
Summary of Pros and Cons *63*
Criteria for Comparison *66*
Recommendations for Different Needs *69*
Conclusion **71**
Recap of Importance of Avoiding Harmful Substances .. *71*
Final Thoughts and Recommendations *73*
Potential References **76**

Introduction

In today's world, we are constantly exposed to a variety of substances that can have harmful effects on our health. These substances, often referred to as toxins, can come from a variety of sources including the food we eat, the air we breathe, and the products we use. While it's impossible to completely eliminate our exposure to toxins, it's important to take steps to minimize our exposure to these harmful substances to improve our health and well-being.

Importance of Avoiding Harmful Substances

Toxins are substances that have the potential to harm our bodies in a variety of ways. Exposure to toxins can lead to a range of health issues including allergies, asthma, cancer, reproductive problems, and even death. Toxins can also have a negative impact on our mental health, contributing to issues such as depression and anxiety.

One of the most significant concerns regarding toxins is their potential to cause chronic diseases. Many toxins are known carcinogens, meaning they have the potential to cause cancer. In fact, it's estimated that up to 90% of all cancer cases are caused by environmental factors such as exposure to toxins.

Toxins can also have a cumulative effect on our bodies, meaning that small exposures over time can add up to cause significant harm. This is particularly concerning when it comes to children, as they are more vulnerable to the harmful effects of toxins and their developing bodies can be impacted by even small exposures.

In addition to the health risks associated with toxins, there are also significant economic costs. Health care costs associated with exposure to toxins are estimated to be in the billions of dollars each year. Additionally, exposure to toxins can impact productivity and result in lost workdays.

By taking steps to minimize our exposure to toxins, we can not only improve our individual health, but also reduce the economic burden associated with environmental toxins.

Overall, the importance of avoiding harmful substances cannot be overstated. It's essential that we take steps to reduce our exposure to toxins in order to protect our health and well-being. In the following chapters, we will explore common toxins and their effects, methods for tracking and reducing exposure, tips for toxin-free living, and the latest technology to help us live a toxin-free life.

Purpose of the Book

The purpose of this book is to provide a comprehensive guide to help readers minimize their exposure to harmful substances and live a toxin-free life. The book will explore the various types of toxins, their effects on our health, and methods for tracking and reducing our exposure. It will also provide tips for living a toxin-free life, including alternative products and services, DIY solutions, and the latest technology.

The purpose of this book is to educate readers on the importance of avoiding harmful substances and provide practical solutions to help them achieve a toxin-free life. In today's world, we are exposed to a variety of substances that can have harmful effects on our health. From the food we eat to the products we use, toxins are all around us. This book will provide readers with the knowledge and tools they need to minimize their exposure to toxins and protect their health.

The book is intended for a wide range of readers, from those who are just beginning to learn about toxins and their effects, to those who are already familiar with the topic and looking for practical solutions. It will provide clear and concise information on common toxins and their effects, as well as methods for tracking and reducing exposure.

The book is also intended to serve as a practical guide for those who are interested in living a toxin-free life. It will provide tips and tricks for avoiding toxins in everyday life, as well as alternative products and services that can help readers reduce their exposure. Additionally, the book will explore the latest technology for living a toxin-free life, including popular brands and devices.

Overall, the purpose of this book is to provide readers with the knowledge and tools they need to protect their health and well-being by minimizing their exposure to harmful substances. By following the practical solutions and advice provided in this book, readers can take control of their health and live a happier, healthier life.

Overview of Toxins and How They Affect Health

Toxins are substances that can have harmful effects on our health. They can be found in a variety of products and substances, including food, water, air, household products, and personal care items. Exposure to toxins can lead to a range of health problems, from minor irritations to serious illnesses.

Toxins can be divided into several categories, including chemical toxins, biological toxins, and environmental toxins. Chemical toxins are substances that are created through human activities, such as industrial processes, and can include heavy metals, pesticides, and synthetic chemicals. Biological toxins are substances that are created by living organisms, such as bacteria, viruses, and fungi. Environmental toxins include pollutants in the air, water, and soil, such as lead and mercury.

How Toxins Affect Health

Toxins can affect our health in a variety of ways, depending on the type and level of exposure. Some toxins can have immediate effects, such as skin irritations or respiratory problems, while others can have long-term effects, such as cancer or neurological disorders. Additionally, some toxins can accumulate in the body over time, leading to chronic health problems.

Exposure to toxins can occur through various routes, including ingestion, inhalation, and absorption through the skin. Some of the most common health effects of exposure to toxins include respiratory problems, skin irritations, headaches, and fatigue. In more severe cases, exposure to toxins can lead to cancer, organ damage, or death.

Preventing Exposure to Toxins

Preventing exposure to toxins is important for maintaining good health. There are several steps that individuals can take to minimize their exposure to toxins, including avoiding processed foods, choosing organic produce, using natural cleaning and personal care products, and reducing exposure to pollutants in the air and water. Additionally, using technology such as air purifiers, water filters, and smart home systems can help individuals monitor and reduce their exposure to toxins in their environment.

Conclusion

In conclusion, toxins are substances that can have harmful effects on our health. They can be found in a wide range of products and substances, and exposure to toxins can lead to a variety of health problems. By understanding the types of toxins and how they can affect our health, individuals can take steps to minimize their exposure and protect their health. The following chapters will provide more detailed information on common toxins, methods for tracking and reducing exposure, tips for living a toxin-free life, and the latest technology for toxin-free living.

Chapter 1: Common Toxins and Their Effects

List and Description of Common Toxins

Toxins are substances that can have harmful effects on our health, and they can be found in a wide range of products and substances in our daily lives. Understanding the types of toxins that we are exposed to and their effects on our health is crucial for making informed decisions about our lifestyles and protecting our health. In this chapter, we will provide a list and description of common toxins, their sources of exposure, and their health effects.

Heavy Metals

Heavy metals are toxic elements that are commonly found in our environment, including lead, mercury, arsenic, cadmium, and aluminum. These metals can accumulate in the body over time, leading to chronic health problems, such as neurological disorders, kidney damage, and cancer.

Lead is a particularly dangerous heavy metal that can be found in old paint, soil, and contaminated water. Exposure to lead can cause developmental delays, behavioral problems, and cognitive impairments, particularly in children.

Mercury is another dangerous heavy metal that can be found in fish, dental fillings, and certain medications.

Exposure to mercury can cause neurological problems, such as tremors, memory loss, and mood changes.

Pesticides

Pesticides are chemicals that are used to kill pests, such as insects and weeds, and are commonly found in our food, water, and environment. Exposure to pesticides can cause a range of health problems, including cancer, birth defects, and neurological problems.

Organophosphate pesticides, in particular, are known to be toxic to the nervous system, and exposure to these chemicals has been linked to learning disabilities, developmental delays, and behavioral problems in children.

Synthetic Chemicals

Synthetic chemicals, including phthalates, bisphenol A (BPA), and perfluorinated compounds (PFCs), are used in a wide range of products, including plastics, food packaging, and personal care items. These chemicals can disrupt hormonal balance, leading to a range of health problems, including reproductive problems, developmental delays, and cancer.

Phthalates are used in plastics, personal care products, and food packaging and can affect the development of the reproductive system, particularly in males.

BPA is a chemical found in plastics, such as water bottles, and can interfere with hormone levels, leading to reproductive problems and other health issues.

PFCs are found in products such as non-stick cookware and stain-resistant fabrics and can accumulate in the body over time, leading to liver damage, hormonal disruption, and other health problems.

Air Pollutants

Air pollutants, including particulate matter, ozone, and sulfur dioxide, can be found in both outdoor and indoor air and can cause respiratory problems, cardiovascular disease, and other health problems.

Particulate matter, which can be generated by power plants and vehicle exhaust, can cause lung irritation, aggravate asthma, and increase the risk of heart disease.

Ozone, which is formed by the interaction of sunlight and pollutants, can cause respiratory problems, including coughing and shortness of breath.

Sulfur dioxide, which is released by power plants and other industrial sources, can cause respiratory problems, including bronchitis and asthma.

Conclusion

In conclusion, exposure to toxins can have serious health effects, and it is important to be aware of the types of toxins that we are exposed to and how to minimize that exposure. Heavy metals, pesticides, synthetic chemicals, and air pollutants are just a few examples of common toxins that we encounter in our daily lives. In the following chapters, we will explore methods for tracking and reducing exposure to these toxins and tips for living a toxin-free life.

Health Effects of Exposure

Exposure to toxins can have a range of negative health effects, ranging from acute symptoms to chronic illnesses that develop over time. In this section, we will explore the various health effects of exposure to common toxins.

1. Heavy Metals

Heavy metals are toxic elements that can accumulate in the body over time. Exposure to heavy metals can lead to a range of health effects, including:

Neurological problems: Exposure to heavy metals such as lead, mercury, and cadmium can cause a range of neurological problems, including headaches, dizziness, tremors, and seizures. Prolonged exposure can also lead to more serious neurological problems such as Parkinson's disease and Alzheimer's disease.

Cardiovascular problems: Heavy metal exposure has been linked to an increased risk of heart disease, stroke, and hypertension. Heavy metals can also interfere with the body's ability to produce red blood cells, which can lead to anemia.

Kidney damage: Many heavy metals are toxic to the kidneys and can cause damage to these vital organs. Lead, cadmium, and mercury are particularly harmful to the kidneys, and prolonged exposure can lead to kidney failure.

2. Pesticides

Pesticides are chemicals used to kill pests such as insects, rodents, and weeds. Exposure to pesticides can have a range of health effects, including:

Respiratory problems: Pesticides can irritate the lungs and cause breathing problems. In some cases, exposure to pesticides can lead to asthma or other chronic respiratory illnesses.

Skin irritation: Pesticides can irritate the skin, causing rashes, blisters, and other skin problems. Prolonged exposure can lead to more serious skin problems such as skin cancer.

Neurological problems: Some pesticides are toxic to the nervous system and can cause neurological problems such as headaches, dizziness, and tremors. Long-term exposure can also lead to more serious neurological problems such as Parkinson's disease and Alzheimer's disease.

3. Volatile Organic Compounds (VOCs)

Volatile organic compounds (VOCs) are chemicals that can evaporate into the air at room temperature. Exposure to VOCs can have a range of health effects, including:

Respiratory problems: VOCs can irritate the lungs and cause breathing problems. Prolonged exposure to high levels of VOCs can lead to chronic respiratory problems such as asthma.

Eye and nose irritation: Exposure to VOCs can cause eye and nose irritation, including burning, itching, and watering of the eyes, as well as a runny nose.

Headaches and dizziness: VOCs can cause headaches, dizziness, and fatigue. Prolonged exposure to high levels of VOCs can also cause nausea and vomiting.

4. Endocrine Disruptors

Endocrine disruptors are chemicals that can interfere with the body's hormone system. Exposure to endocrine disruptors can have a range of health effects, including:

Reproductive problems: Endocrine disruptors can interfere with reproductive function, leading to infertility, menstrual problems, and other reproductive health issues.

Developmental problems: Exposure to endocrine disruptors during pregnancy can interfere with fetal development, leading to birth defects and other developmental problems.

Cancer: Some endocrine disruptors have been linked to an increased risk of certain types of cancer, including breast cancer and prostate cancer.

These are just a few examples of the health effects of exposure to common toxins. It is important to be aware of the potential health risks of exposure to toxins and take steps to minimize your exposure in order to protect your health.

Sources of Exposure

Toxins can enter our bodies in a variety of ways, and many everyday products and activities can be sources of exposure. The following are some common sources of exposure to toxins:

1. Air pollution: Air pollution is a major source of exposure to toxins, especially in urban areas. Particulate matter, carbon monoxide, and nitrogen oxides are among the most common pollutants that can cause respiratory and other health problems.

2. Water pollution: Water pollution can also expose people to toxins. Chemicals and heavy metals such as lead, mercury, and arsenic can contaminate drinking water sources.

3. Food and beverages: Many foods and beverages can contain toxins, either naturally or due to contamination during production or processing. Examples include mercury in fish, pesticides on produce, and artificial sweeteners in soda.

4. Personal care products: Many personal care products such as shampoo, lotion, and makeup can contain harmful chemicals. For example, phthalates, parabens, and formaldehyde are commonly used in personal care products and have been linked to health problems.

5. Cleaning products: Cleaning products can also contain toxins that can be harmful when inhaled or touched. Examples include ammonia, bleach, and other harsh chemicals.

6. Household items: Many household items, such as furniture, carpet, and electronics, can contain toxins. For example, flame retardants and other chemicals used in furniture and electronics can be harmful when they enter the environment.

7. Workplace exposure: Many workers are exposed to toxins on the job, especially in industries such as mining, manufacturing, and agriculture. Workers may be exposed to chemicals such as lead, asbestos, and pesticides, which can cause serious health problems.

8. Environmental exposure: Toxins can also be present in the environment, such as in soil, air, or water, which can affect people living in the area.

It is important to note that exposure to toxins is not always immediately obvious. Some toxins may accumulate in the body over time, leading to health problems that may not be immediately apparent. Additionally, different people may have different levels of susceptibility to toxins, depending on factors such as age, genetics, and overall health.

Overall, understanding the sources of exposure to toxins is an important step in taking control of your health and reducing your risk of exposure. By being aware of the potential sources of exposure in your environment, you can take steps to minimize your risk and protect your health.

Chapter 2: Tracking Your Exposure
Methods for Tracking Exposure

Tracking your exposure to toxins is an important first step in reducing your risk of exposure and protecting your health. By identifying the sources and levels of toxins in your environment, you can take action to minimize your exposure and make informed decisions about the products you use and the activities you engage in. The following are some methods for tracking exposure to toxins:

1. Biomonitoring: Biomonitoring is the process of measuring the levels of chemicals and toxins in a person's blood, urine, or other bodily fluids. This method can provide an accurate picture of a person's exposure to specific chemicals, but it is typically only used for a limited number of chemicals and can be expensive.

2. Environmental monitoring: Environmental monitoring involves measuring the levels of toxins in the air, water, soil, or other environmental samples. This method can help identify sources of exposure in a particular area, but it may not provide information on a person's actual exposure.

3. Consumer product testing: Consumer product testing involves analyzing products such as food, personal care products, and cleaning products for the presence of

toxins. This method can help identify specific products that may be a source of exposure, but it does not provide information on a person's actual exposure.

4. Personal exposure monitoring: Personal exposure monitoring involves using wearable devices or other technology to measure a person's exposure to toxins in real-time. This method can provide immediate feedback on a person's exposure levels and can be used to identify specific activities or products that may be a source of exposure.

5. Questionnaires and surveys: Questionnaires and surveys can be used to gather information on a person's activities, lifestyle, and use of specific products. This method can help identify potential sources of exposure and can be used to guide further testing or monitoring.

6. Electronic health records: Electronic health records (EHRs) can also be used to track a person's exposure to toxins over time. By collecting data on a person's medical history, medications, and other factors, EHRs can help identify patterns and potential sources of exposure.

Each of these methods has its own advantages and limitations, and the most appropriate method will depend on the specific situation and the information needed. For example, biomonitoring may be most appropriate for individuals who work in high-risk occupations, while personal exposure monitoring may be more appropriate for identifying sources of exposure in the home or community.

Overall, tracking your exposure to toxins is an important step in taking control of your health and reducing your risk of exposure. By using one or more of these methods, you can identify potential sources of exposure and take action to minimize your risk and protect your health.

Pros and Cons

When it comes to tracking your exposure to toxins, there are various methods available, each with its own set of pros and cons. Understanding these advantages and disadvantages can help you decide which method is right for you. In this section, we will explore the pros and cons of some of the most popular methods for tracking your exposure to toxins.

1. Biological Monitoring Biological monitoring involves analyzing biological samples such as blood, urine, or hair to detect the presence of toxins. The primary advantage of this method is that it provides a direct measurement of the amount of a toxin that has been absorbed into the body. It can also identify the source of the exposure, which can be helpful in identifying ways to reduce exposure in the future. However, biological monitoring can be invasive and uncomfortable, and it may not provide an accurate representation of the total amount of exposure.

2. Environmental Monitoring Environmental monitoring involves testing the air, water, soil, or other environmental factors for the presence of toxins. This method can provide a broader picture of the types and levels of toxins present in a given environment. It can be useful for identifying potential sources of exposure and for

determining if exposure levels are within safe limits. However, environmental monitoring can be expensive, and it may not capture all sources of exposure.

3. Wearable Sensors Wearable sensors are small devices that can be worn on the body and can track exposure to a range of toxins, including volatile organic compounds, heavy metals, and particulate matter. The main advantage of wearable sensors is that they provide real-time data on exposure levels. They are also non-invasive and can be worn throughout the day. However, wearable sensors may not be as accurate as other methods of tracking exposure, and they may not capture all sources of exposure.

4. Smartphone Apps Smartphone apps are becoming increasingly popular for tracking exposure to toxins. These apps use GPS to track the user's location and provide information on the types and levels of toxins present in the surrounding environment. They can also provide information on potential sources of exposure and ways to reduce exposure. The main advantage of smartphone apps is their ease of use and accessibility. However, they may not be as accurate as other methods of tracking exposure, and they may not capture all sources of exposure.

5. Personal Monitoring Devices Personal monitoring devices are small devices that can be worn on the body and

can measure exposure to specific toxins. These devices can provide real-time data on exposure levels and can be useful for identifying potential sources of exposure. They are also non-invasive and can be worn throughout the day. However, personal monitoring devices can be expensive, and they may not capture all sources of exposure.

In conclusion, each method of tracking exposure to toxins has its own set of advantages and disadvantages. It's important to understand these pros and cons before deciding which method is right for you. It's also important to remember that no single method can capture all sources of exposure, and that a combination of methods may be needed for a more comprehensive understanding of your exposure to toxins.

Popular Brands and Devices

In the previous section, we discussed the various methods for tracking your exposure to harmful toxins. In this section, we will explore some of the popular brands and devices available in the market for tracking exposure. As more and more people become aware of the dangers of toxins, the demand for tracking devices has increased. In response, numerous companies have developed tracking tools that are aimed at helping individuals monitor their exposure to toxins.

1. Environmental Working Group (EWG) Healthy Living App

The EWG Healthy Living App is a free tool that enables users to scan barcodes and determine the safety of different products. The app has a database of over 120,000 products, which allows users to make informed decisions about the products they purchase. The app uses a rating system based on the toxicity of the ingredients, and users can see detailed information about each product's ingredients.

Pros:

Free to use

Large database of products

Simple to use

Cons:

Not all products are included in the database

May not have information on all the ingredients

2. My Chemical-Free House

My Chemical-Free House is a website that provides information on how to create a chemical-free home. The website includes a list of recommended products and materials that are safe to use. The website also provides information on the dangers of different types of chemicals and how to avoid them.

Pros:

Comprehensive information on how to create a chemical-free home

Detailed information on different chemicals and their dangers

Cons:

Not a tracking tool

Information is limited to creating a chemical-free home

3. AirVisual Pro

The AirVisual Pro is a device that measures air quality and tracks the levels of different toxins in the air. The device provides real-time data on air quality and can be connected to a smartphone app that allows users to track their exposure to toxins.

Pros:

Provides real-time data on air quality

Can track exposure to toxins over time

Easy to use

Cons:

Expensive

Only tracks air quality and does not provide information on other sources of exposure

4. Gaiam Wellness Meditation Chair

The Gaiam Wellness Meditation Chair is a device that helps to reduce exposure to electromagnetic radiation. The chair has a grounding pad that is designed to reduce the amount of radiation absorbed by the body.

Pros:

Helps to reduce exposure to electromagnetic radiation

Comfortable to use

Cons:

Only reduces exposure to electromagnetic radiation

Expensive

5. 3M LeadCheck Swabs

The 3M LeadCheck Swabs are a simple and inexpensive tool for testing for lead. The swabs can be used to test for lead on any surface and provide results within 30 seconds.

Pros:

Inexpensive

Easy to use

Provides quick results

Cons:

Only tests for lead

May not be accurate in all cases

6. Water Testing Kits

Water testing kits are available from a variety of companies and can be used to test for different toxins in the water. Some water testing kits are designed to test for lead, while others are designed to test for other toxins such as arsenic, nitrates, and pesticides.

Pros:

Easy to use

Inexpensive

Provides quick results

Cons:

Only tests for specific toxins

May not be accurate in all cases

Conclusion:

The above are just a few examples of popular brands and devices available for tracking exposure to toxins. As the demand for these devices increases, we can expect to see more products and tools becoming available. It is important to do your research and choose the tools that are best suited to your needs and budget. Remember that while tracking devices can be helpful, they are not a substitute for avoiding exposure to toxins in your environment. It's essential to combine tracking with proactive measures to reduce exposure, such as choosing non-toxic products and making lifestyle changes that prioritize toxin-free living. While tracking your exposure can provide valuable insights into your exposure patterns, it's important to use this information to take action to reduce your exposure to harmful substances. With the right tools and a commitment to a toxin-free lifestyle, you can take control of your health and well-being, and reduce your risk of developing a range of health problems associated with exposure to toxins.

Chapter 3: Reducing Your Exposure
Methods for Reducing Exposure

Exposure to toxins can have a significant impact on your health, so it's important to take steps to reduce your exposure as much as possible. While it's impossible to completely avoid all toxins, there are many methods and techniques you can use to significantly reduce your exposure. In this chapter, we'll explore some of the most effective methods for reducing your exposure to toxins.

1. Choosing non-toxic products

One of the most effective ways to reduce your exposure to toxins is to choose non-toxic products whenever possible. This can include everything from personal care products to household cleaners to food and beverages. Look for products that are made from natural or organic ingredients, and avoid products that contain harmful chemicals such as phthalates, parabens, and triclosan.

2. Improving indoor air quality

Indoor air quality can have a significant impact on your health, as many harmful toxins can be found in indoor air. To reduce your exposure to indoor air toxins, consider using an air purifier to remove harmful particles from the air. You can also improve indoor air quality by regularly cleaning your home, ventilating your home by opening windows and using exhaust fans, and avoiding the use of products that release harmful chemicals into the air.

3. Eating a healthy diet

The food you eat can also have a significant impact on your exposure to toxins. To reduce your exposure to toxins through your diet, consider eating a diet that is rich in fruits and vegetables, as well as other nutrient-dense foods. Avoid processed foods, which can be loaded with artificial additives and preservatives, and choose organic foods whenever possible, which are less likely to contain harmful pesticides and other chemicals.

4. Filtering your water

Water can also contain harmful toxins, including heavy metals and other contaminants. To reduce your exposure to these toxins, consider using a water filter to remove harmful particles from your drinking water. There are many different types of water filters available, including countertop and under-sink models, as well as portable water filters that you can take with you on the go.

5. Reducing plastic use

Plastic is a ubiquitous material that is found in many products and packaging materials. Unfortunately, plastic can also contain harmful chemicals that can leach into food and beverages, and can also be harmful to the environment. To reduce your exposure to plastic toxins, consider using alternatives to plastic whenever possible, such as glass, stainless steel, or silicone. You can also reduce your use of plastic by choosing products with minimal packaging and by using reusable shopping bags and containers.

6. Choosing safer cleaning products

Many household cleaning products contain harmful chemicals that can be harmful to your health. To reduce your exposure to these toxins, consider using safer cleaning products that are made from natural or organic ingredients. You can also make your own cleaning products using simple ingredients such as vinegar, baking soda, and lemon juice.

7. Using natural pest control methods

Pesticides and other chemical treatments can be harmful to your health and can also have a negative impact on the environment. To reduce your exposure to these toxins, consider using natural pest control methods such as essential oils, diatomaceous earth, and other natural remedies. You can also use traps and barriers to prevent pests from entering your home in the first place.

8. Making lifestyle changes

Finally, making lifestyle changes can also be an effective way to reduce your exposure to toxins. This can include things like quitting smoking, reducing alcohol consumption, and getting regular exercise. By taking care of your overall health, you can reduce your risk of developing health problems associated with exposure to toxins.

*****

Overall, there are many methods for reducing your exposure to toxins, and it's important to use a combination of methods to achieve the best results. By making simple changes to your daily routines and habits, you can significantly reduce your exposure to harmful substances. Some common methods for reducing exposure to toxins include:

1. Switching to natural and organic products: One of the most effective ways to reduce your exposure to toxins is by choosing natural and organic products, such as food, personal care products, cleaning supplies, and household items. These products are free from harmful chemicals, pesticides, and other toxins that can be found in conventional products.

2. Improving indoor air quality: Indoor air pollution can be a major source of toxins in the home. To reduce exposure, it's important to improve indoor air quality by keeping your home well-ventilated, using air purifiers, and avoiding the use of harmful chemicals such as air fresheners and synthetic fragrances.

3. Eating a healthy diet: A healthy diet is essential for reducing your exposure to toxins. By eating a diet rich in fruits, vegetables, whole grains, and lean protein, you can improve your overall health and reduce your exposure to harmful chemicals found in processed and fast foods.

4. Drinking clean water: Clean drinking water is essential for good health. To reduce your exposure to toxins in water, it's important to drink filtered or purified water that is free from contaminants such as lead, chlorine, and other harmful chemicals.

5. Using natural remedies: Natural remedies, such as essential oils, herbs, and supplements, can be effective for reducing exposure to toxins. For example, using essential oils for cleaning or personal care can be a great way to reduce your exposure to harmful chemicals found in conventional cleaning and personal care products.

6. Avoiding exposure to radiation: Exposure to radiation, whether from natural or man-made sources, can be harmful to your health. To reduce your exposure, it's important to avoid unnecessary medical tests that use radiation, such as X-rays and CT scans, and to limit your exposure to sources of radiation in the environment.

By incorporating these methods into your daily routine, you can significantly reduce your exposure to toxins and improve your overall health and well-being.

Pros and Cons

When it comes to reducing your exposure to toxins, there are a variety of methods you can use. Each method has its own set of advantages and disadvantages. Here are some of the most common pros and cons to consider:

1. Natural Products:

Natural products, such as vinegar and baking soda, are affordable, readily available, and environmentally friendly. They can be used for a variety of purposes, including cleaning, pest control, and personal care. However, they may not be as effective as some commercial products, and they may not have a long shelf life.

2. Commercial Products:

Commercial products are often highly effective and widely available. They may also be designed for specific purposes, such as killing bacteria or removing stains. However, they can be expensive, and many contain toxic chemicals that can be harmful to your health and the environment.

3. Lifestyle Changes:

Lifestyle changes, such as eating a healthy diet and exercising regularly, can help reduce your exposure to toxins. They can also improve your overall health and well-being.

However, they can be difficult to maintain, and they may not be enough to eliminate all sources of toxins.

4. Air Purifiers:

Air purifiers can help remove toxins and pollutants from the air in your home or office. They can be especially useful for people with allergies or respiratory problems. However, they can be expensive to purchase and operate, and they may not be effective against all types of pollutants.

5. Water Filters:

Water filters can help remove toxins and contaminants from your drinking water. They can also improve the taste and smell of your water. However, they can be expensive, and they may not be effective against all types of toxins.

6. Clothing and Bedding:

Clothing and bedding made from natural materials, such as cotton and wool, are often less likely to contain toxins than synthetic materials. However, they can be more expensive, and they may require special care.

7. Indoor Plants:

Indoor plants can help improve the air quality in your home or office by removing toxins from the air. They can also be aesthetically pleasing. However, they require care and attention, and they may not be effective against all types of toxins.

Overall, the key to reducing your exposure to toxins is to use a combination of methods that work best for your lifestyle, budget, and preferences. It's also important to do your research and choose products and methods that are safe and effective.

Popular Brands and Devices

When it comes to reducing exposure to toxins, there are many popular brands and devices available that can help. Here are some examples:

1. Air Purifiers: Air purifiers are designed to remove harmful particles and pollutants from the air, such as mold, dust, and pet dander. Some popular brands include HEPA filters from brands like Honeywell and Coway, and Molekule air purifiers.

2. Water Filters: Water filters can help to remove contaminants from tap water, such as lead, chlorine, and pesticides. Popular brands include Brita, PUR, and ZeroWater.

3. Organic Foods: Organic foods are grown without the use of synthetic pesticides and fertilizers, making them a popular choice for those looking to reduce their exposure to toxins in their diet. Some popular organic food brands include Stonyfield Farms, Amy's Kitchen, and Annie's Homegrown.

4. Non-Toxic Cleaning Products: Cleaning products can be a significant source of toxic exposure in the home. Non-toxic cleaning products, such as those from brands like Seventh Generation and Method, can help to reduce exposure to harmful chemicals like ammonia and bleach.

5. Natural Personal Care Products: Personal care products, including shampoo, conditioner, lotion, and deodorant, can also contain harmful chemicals. Natural personal care products, such as those from brands like Burt's Bees and Dr. Bronner's, can be a safer alternative.

6. Low VOC Paint: Many traditional paints contain volatile organic compounds (VOCs) that can release harmful chemicals into the air. Low VOC paint, such as those from brands like Benjamin Moore and Sherwin-Williams, can help to reduce exposure.

7. EMF Protection Devices: Electromagnetic fields (EMFs) are generated by electronic devices such as cell phones and Wi-Fi routers. EMF protection devices, such as shields and stickers, claim to reduce exposure to harmful EMF radiation.

It's important to note that while these products can be helpful in reducing exposure to toxins, they should not be relied on as the sole method of protection. It's still essential to take other steps, such as avoiding harmful chemicals whenever possible and incorporating healthy habits into your daily routine.

Chapter 4: Toxin-Free Living

Tips and Tricks for Living a Toxin-Free Life

Living a toxin-free life can seem like a daunting task, but it is achievable with the right mindset and strategies. Here are some tips and tricks to help you get started:

1. Eat Organic: Choosing organic foods is an easy way to avoid toxins in your diet. Organic farming practices prohibit the use of synthetic pesticides and fertilizers, making organic foods a healthier choice.

2. Read Labels: Many household and personal care products contain harmful toxins. Make it a habit to read labels and choose products with natural and non-toxic ingredients.

3. Purify Your Air: Indoor air can be even more polluted than outdoor air. Use air-purifying plants, air filters, and open windows to improve the air quality in your home.

4. Avoid Plastic: Many plastics contain toxic chemicals that can leach into food and drinks. Use glass or stainless steel containers whenever possible.

5. Use Natural Cleaning Products: Many household cleaning products contain harsh chemicals that can be harmful to your health. Use natural cleaning products or make your own using simple ingredients like vinegar, baking soda, and lemon juice.

6. Exercise: Exercise helps to flush toxins from your body through sweat and improved circulation. Aim to get regular physical activity to support your body's natural detoxification process.

7. Get Enough Sleep: Adequate sleep is essential for overall health and wellbeing. It allows your body to rest and repair, including the natural detoxification process that occurs during sleep.

8. Practice Mindfulness: Stress can have a negative impact on your health and contribute to toxin buildup in the body. Practice mindfulness techniques like meditation and yoga to reduce stress and improve overall health.

9. Use Natural Pest Control: Many conventional pest control products contain toxic chemicals that can be harmful to human health. Use natural pest control methods like diatomaceous earth, essential oils, and insect traps.

10. Filter Your Water: Tap water can contain toxins like chlorine, lead, and fluoride. Use a high-quality water filter to remove these contaminants and provide your family with safe and clean drinking water.

By incorporating these tips and tricks into your daily routine, you can take important steps towards living a toxin-free life. Remember, small changes can make a big difference in your health and wellbeing.

Alternative Products and Services

When it comes to living a toxin-free life, it's important to be mindful of the products and services we use on a daily basis. While many common household items and personal care products contain harmful chemicals and toxins, there are alternative options available that can help reduce exposure.

Here are some alternative products and services to consider:

1. Natural Cleaning Products: Many cleaning products contain harsh chemicals and toxins that can be harmful to your health. Consider using natural cleaning products instead, such as vinegar, baking soda, and essential oils. These alternatives can be just as effective and are much safer for you and the environment.

2. Organic Food: Conventionally grown fruits and vegetables are often treated with pesticides and herbicides, which can leave harmful residues. Choosing organic food can help reduce your exposure to these toxins. You can also consider growing your own produce, either indoors or in a backyard garden.

3. Non-Toxic Personal Care Products: Many personal care products, such as shampoos, soaps, and lotions, contain chemicals that can be harmful to your health. Look for

products that are labeled as "natural" or "organic" and avoid those that contain phthalates, parabens, and synthetic fragrances.

4. Water Filtration Systems: Tap water can contain harmful chemicals and toxins, such as chlorine and fluoride. Investing in a water filtration system can help remove these impurities and ensure that you are drinking clean, safe water.

5. Alternative Medicine: There are many alternative medicine practices that can help support your health and reduce your exposure to toxins. Some popular options include acupuncture, herbal medicine, and chiropractic care.

6. Eco-Friendly Home Products: Consider using eco-friendly products in your home, such as recycled paper products, LED light bulbs, and reusable water bottles. These products can help reduce waste and exposure to harmful toxins.

By making small changes to the products and services you use on a daily basis, you can help reduce your exposure to harmful toxins and live a more toxin-free life.

DIY and Homemade Solutions

DIY and homemade solutions can be an effective and affordable way to reduce exposure to toxins in the home. Many common household cleaning products, personal care items, and even food and drinks can contain harmful chemicals. By making your own products using natural and safe ingredients, you can eliminate the risks associated with these products and reduce your overall exposure to toxins. Here are some tips and recipes for creating your own toxin-free products:

1. Cleaning products: Many store-bought cleaning products contain harmful chemicals such as bleach, ammonia, and phthalates. Instead, try making your own cleaning products using natural ingredients such as vinegar, baking soda, and essential oils. For example, mix vinegar and water in a spray bottle for a natural all-purpose cleaner, or use a baking soda and vinegar paste to clean tough stains.

2. Personal care products: Many personal care products such as shampoo, soap, and deodorant contain harmful chemicals such as parabens, phthalates, and triclosan. You can make your own natural personal care products using ingredients such as coconut oil, shea butter, and essential oils. For example, mix coconut oil, baking soda, and essential oils to create a natural deodorant.

3. Food and drink: Many foods and drinks can contain harmful additives such as artificial colors, flavors, and preservatives. By making your own food and drinks using natural ingredients, you can avoid these harmful additives. For example, make your own smoothies using fresh fruit and vegetables, or make your own salad dressing using olive oil and vinegar.

4. Pest control: Many pest control products contain harmful chemicals such as pesticides and insecticides. Instead of using these products, try making your own pest control solutions using natural ingredients such as peppermint oil, garlic, and vinegar. For example, mix peppermint oil and water in a spray bottle to repel ants and other insects.

5. Air fresheners: Many air fresheners contain harmful chemicals such as phthalates and formaldehyde. Instead of using these products, try making your own air fresheners using natural ingredients such as essential oils and baking soda. For example, mix baking soda and essential oils in a jar for a natural air freshener.

Overall, making your own DIY and homemade solutions can be a great way to reduce exposure to toxins in the home. However, it's important to remember that natural ingredients can still be harmful if not used properly, so be sure to do your research and follow instructions carefully when making your own products.

Chapter 5: Technology for Toxin-Free Living
Latest Technology for Living a Toxin-Free Life

In recent years, technology has played an increasingly important role in helping people live a toxin-free life. From air purifiers to water filtration systems, there are a variety of high-tech solutions that can help reduce exposure to harmful toxins. In this chapter, we will explore some of the latest technology for living a toxin-free life.

1. Air Purifiers:

Indoor air pollution is a major health concern, with toxins like volatile organic compounds (VOCs), mold spores, and allergens being major contributors. Air purifiers use a variety of technologies to remove these pollutants from the air, including HEPA filters, activated carbon filters, and ionizers. There are many different brands and models available, with some of the most popular including Blueair, Dyson, and Coway.

2. Water Filtration Systems:

Contaminated drinking water can be a significant source of exposure to toxins like lead, chlorine, and fluoride. Water filtration systems use a variety of technologies to remove these contaminants, including activated carbon filters, reverse osmosis, and ultraviolet sterilization. Popular brands include Brita, PUR, and Aquasana.

3. Smart Home Devices:

Smart home devices allow you to control various aspects of your home environment from your smartphone or tablet. Some of the latest smart home devices are designed to help you live a toxin-free life, including air quality monitors, water quality monitors, and even smart thermostats that can help regulate the temperature and humidity in your home.

4. Non-Toxic Cleaning Products:

Many cleaning products contain harmful toxins like ammonia, bleach, and phthalates. Fortunately, there are a growing number of non-toxic cleaning products available that use natural ingredients like vinegar, lemon, and baking soda. Popular brands include Method, Seventh Generation, and Mrs. Meyer's.

5. Organic and Natural Personal Care Products:

Conventional personal care products like shampoo, soap, and lotion often contain harmful toxins like parabens, phthalates, and synthetic fragrances. Organic and natural personal care products are made with natural, non-toxic ingredients like essential oils and plant extracts. Popular brands include Burt's Bees, Dr. Bronner's, and Alba Botanica.

6. Healthy Home Products:

There are a variety of products available that can help promote a toxin-free home environment, including organic bedding and mattresses, natural pest control products, and eco-friendly paints and flooring. By choosing these products, you can help reduce your exposure to harmful toxins and create a healthier home environment.

In conclusion, technology has brought many innovative solutions to help people live a toxin-free life. By using the latest technology for air purification, water filtration, smart home devices, non-toxic cleaning products, organic and natural personal care products, and healthy home products, it's possible to create a healthy and safe home environment that's free from toxins. As technology continues to evolve, we can expect to see even more advances in the future that will help people live healthier, toxin-free lives.

Pros and Cons

When it comes to using technology for toxin-free living, there are both pros and cons to consider. Some of the advantages of using technology in this context include:

1. Increased accessibility: Technology has made it easier for people to access information about toxins and ways to reduce exposure. With the click of a button, people can access articles, blogs, and forums to learn more about how to live a toxin-free life.

2. Greater convenience: Some technology can help people reduce their exposure to toxins more conveniently. For example, smart home systems can help people monitor air quality and adjust their home's air filtration system as needed.

3. More accurate tracking: Certain technology devices, such as wearable sensors or air quality monitors, can provide more accurate and detailed data about exposure to toxins.

4. Potential cost savings: Investing in technology may lead to long-term cost savings if it helps people avoid exposure to toxins and prevent health problems.

However, there are also some potential disadvantages to using technology for toxin-free living, including:

1. High cost: Some technology devices can be expensive, which may make them less accessible to people with limited budgets.

2. Dependence on technology: Relying too heavily on technology to reduce exposure to toxins may make people less aware of other ways to minimize exposure.

3. Information overload: With so much information available online, it can be overwhelming to sort through it all and determine which sources are reliable.

4. Limited effectiveness: Some technology devices may not be effective in reducing exposure to certain types of toxins or in certain environments.

It's important for individuals to weigh the pros and cons of using technology in their efforts to live a toxin-free life and determine what works best for their specific needs and circumstances.

Popular Brands and Devices

With the rise in interest in toxin-free living and the increasing awareness of the negative health effects of exposure to toxins, more and more companies are offering products that help individuals reduce their exposure to harmful substances. Here are some popular brands and devices that are available on the market.

1. Air Purifiers

a. Blueair: Blueair is a Swedish company that offers a range of air purifiers. Their products are designed to remove a wide range of pollutants, including allergens, viruses, and bacteria.

b. Coway: Coway is a Korean company that offers air purifiers that use a multi-stage filtration system to remove pollutants from the air. Their products also come with a mobile app that allows users to monitor air quality and control the device remotely.

c. Dyson: Dyson is a British company that offers a range of air purifiers. Their products use a unique filtration system that captures ultrafine particles as small as 0.1 microns.

2. Water Filters

a. Berkey: Berkey is an American company that offers water filtration systems. Their products use a gravity-fed system to remove a wide range of contaminants from water, including bacteria, viruses, and chemicals.

b. Brita: Brita is a German company that offers water filters that use activated carbon to remove contaminants from water. Their products are designed for use with tap water.

c. ZeroWater: ZeroWater is an American company that offers water filters that use a five-stage filtration system to remove impurities from water. Their products are designed to remove virtually all dissolved solids from water, including lead and other heavy metals.

3. Personal Care Products

a. Beautycounter: Beautycounter is an American company that offers a range of personal care products that are free from harmful chemicals. Their products are formulated without a wide range of substances, including parabens, phthalates, and formaldehyde.

b. Dr. Bronner's: Dr. Bronner's is an American company that offers a range of personal care products that are certified organic and free from synthetic fragrances and preservatives. Their products are also packaged in environmentally friendly materials.

c. The Honest Company: The Honest Company is an American company that offers a range of personal care products that are free from harmful chemicals. Their products are formulated without substances like parabens, phthalates, and synthetic fragrances.

4. Cleaning Products

a. Seventh Generation: Seventh Generation is an American company that offers a range of cleaning products that are free from harmful chemicals. Their products are formulated without substances like phthalates, triclosan, and synthetic fragrances.

b. Mrs. Meyer's: Mrs. Meyer's is an American company that offers a range of cleaning products that are free from harmful chemicals. Their products are formulated without substances like phthalates, chlorine, and formaldehyde.

c. Method: Method is an American company that offers a range of cleaning products that are free from harmful chemicals. Their products are formulated without substances like parabens, phthalates, and triclosan.

5. EMF Protection

a. DefenderShield: DefenderShield is an American company that offers a range of EMF protection products. Their products are designed to block electromagnetic radiation emitted by electronic devices.

b. SafeSleeve: SafeSleeve is an American company that offers EMF protection products for electronic devices. Their products are designed to block up to 99% of electromagnetic radiation emitted by devices like smartphones and laptops.

c. TESLA Gold Series Plug-in: The TESLA Gold Series Plug-in is a product offered by a British company called Aires. It is designed to reduce the harmful effects of electromagnetic radiation emitted by electronics and appliances. The device uses patented Tesla technology to protect against electromagnetic radiation and create a more harmonious living environment. The TESLA Gold Series Plug-in is an affordable and easy-to-use device that can be plugged into any electrical outlet in your home or office.

d. Blueair Blue Pure 411 Air Purifier: The Blueair Blue Pure 411 Air Purifier is a popular brand of air purifier that is designed to remove harmful pollutants from the air. It uses a combination of mechanical and electrostatic filtration to capture particles as small as 0.1 microns. The Blueair Blue Pure 411 Air Purifier is a small, lightweight device that can be easily moved from room to room.

e. Berkey Water Filter: The Berkey Water Filter is a popular brand of water filter that is designed to remove harmful contaminants from drinking water. It uses a combination of activated carbon and ion exchange to remove impurities such as chlorine, lead, and bacteria. The Berkey Water Filter is available in a range of sizes and is a great option for those who want to filter their water without relying on bottled water.

As technology continues to advance, we can expect to see more products and devices designed to help us live a toxin-free life. While these products can be helpful, it's important to remember that they are not a substitute for making lifestyle changes that reduce our exposure to toxins. By using a combination of technology and lifestyle changes, we can create a healthier and more harmonious living environment for ourselves and our families.

Chapter 6: Comparing and Contrasting Methods
Summary of Pros and Cons

In the previous chapters, we have explored various methods for tracking, reducing, and eliminating toxins in our daily lives. Each method has its own advantages and disadvantages, and it is important to consider these when deciding which methods to use. In this chapter, we will summarize the pros and cons of each method and compare and contrast them to help you make informed decisions.

Tracking Methods:

1. Personal Air Quality Monitors: Pros - provide real-time data on air quality and can identify specific pollutants; Cons - may not capture all pollutants, can be expensive.

2. Water Testing Kits: Pros - provide accurate and detailed results, relatively inexpensive; Cons - may not capture all contaminants, may require laboratory analysis for some tests.

3. Food Testing Kits: Pros - provide detailed results, can identify specific toxins; Cons - may be expensive and time-consuming, may not capture all toxins.

4. Personal Toxin Exposure Monitors: Pros - provide real-time data on toxin exposure, can help identify sources of exposure; Cons - may be expensive, may not capture all toxins.

Reducing Methods:

1. Ventilation: Pros - can improve air quality and reduce exposure to pollutants; Cons - may not be effective for all pollutants, may increase energy costs.

2. Cleaning: Pros - can remove pollutants from surfaces, can improve indoor air quality; Cons - may not be effective for all pollutants, may require the use of cleaning products that contain toxins.

3. Filters: Pros - can remove pollutants from air and water, relatively inexpensive; Cons - may not capture all pollutants, may require frequent replacement.

4. Personal Protective Equipment: Pros - can reduce exposure to toxins, can be effective for specific activities; Cons - may be uncomfortable to wear, may not be effective for all activities.

Elimination Methods:

1. Choosing Toxin-Free Products: Pros - reduces exposure to toxins, can be effective for specific activities; Cons - may be more expensive, may not be available in all areas.

2. Alternative Solutions: Pros - can be effective and affordable, can eliminate the need for products that contain toxins; Cons - may require more effort to use, may not be effective for all activities.

3. Homemade Solutions: Pros - can be effective and affordable, can eliminate the need for products that contain toxins; Cons - may require more effort to use, may not be effective for all activities.

4. Technology Solutions: Pros - can be effective and affordable, can eliminate the need for products that contain toxins; Cons - may be expensive, may require maintenance.

Overall, there are many methods available for tracking, reducing, and eliminating toxins in our daily lives. Each method has its own advantages and disadvantages, and the best approach is to use a combination of methods to achieve the best results. It is important to consider factors such as effectiveness, cost, and convenience when deciding which methods to use. By taking a proactive approach to reducing our exposure to toxins, we can improve our health and well-being.

Criteria for Comparison

When it comes to comparing and contrasting methods for living a toxin-free life, it's important to have clear criteria to assess their effectiveness. Here are some of the most important factors to consider:

1. Efficacy: How effective is the method at reducing exposure to toxins? Does it have scientific evidence to support its claims?

2. Affordability: Is the method affordable and accessible for most people, or is it limited to those with higher incomes or specialized training?

3. Convenience: How easy is it to incorporate the method into daily life? Does it require significant time or effort?

4. Safety: Are there any potential health risks or side effects associated with the method?

5. Environmental Impact: Does the method have a positive or negative impact on the environment? Is it sustainable in the long-term?

6. Personal Preference: Finally, it's important to consider personal preferences and lifestyle factors. Does the method align with personal values and goals? Is it enjoyable and sustainable in the long-term?

*****

By considering these criteria, it's possible to make an informed decision about which methods for living a toxin-free life are most suitable for each individual.

1. Efficacy:

The efficacy of a method is one of the most important criteria to consider when comparing and contrasting methods for living a toxin-free life. It's important to look for scientific evidence to support the claims made by the method. Some methods may be more effective than others at reducing exposure to certain toxins, so it's important to look for research specific to the toxin in question.

2. Affordability:

Affordability is another important factor to consider. Living a toxin-free life should not be limited to those with higher incomes or specialized training. Methods that are more affordable and accessible to a wider range of people are likely to be more effective in reducing overall exposure to toxins.

3. Convenience:

Convenience is another important factor to consider. Some methods may require significant time or effort, which can be challenging to incorporate into daily life. It's important to consider whether the method is easy to incorporate into a daily routine.

4. Safety:

Safety is another important factor to consider when comparing and contrasting methods for living a toxin-free life. It's important to consider whether there are any potential health risks or side effects associated with the method. Some methods may be more suitable for certain individuals or populations, such as pregnant women or those with certain health conditions.

5. Environmental Impact:

Environmental impact is another important factor to consider. Living a toxin-free life should not come at the expense of the environment. It's important to consider whether the method has a positive or negative impact on the environment and whether it is sustainable in the long-term.

6. Personal Preference:

Finally, personal preference is an important factor to consider. It's important to choose methods that align with personal values and goals, and that are enjoyable and sustainable in the long-term. Some methods may be more suitable for certain individuals depending on their lifestyle and preferences.

By considering these criteria, it's possible to make an informed decision about which methods for living a toxin-free life are most suitable for each individual.

Recommendations for Different Needs

In this section, we will provide recommendations for different needs based on the comparison of methods discussed in the previous section. As different individuals have different needs and priorities, it is important to choose the most suitable method for your specific situation.

1. For individuals who are concerned about reducing exposure to toxins in their immediate environment, we recommend using household cleaning products that are free of harmful chemicals, using a high-quality air purifier to remove airborne pollutants, and ensuring that ventilation in the home is adequate.

2. For individuals who are concerned about exposure to toxins through their diet, we recommend choosing organic produce whenever possible and reducing the consumption of processed foods. It is also important to be aware of the potential sources of toxins in the environment, such as water and air pollution, and to take steps to minimize exposure to these sources.

3. For individuals who are concerned about the effects of electromagnetic radiation on their health, we recommend using devices that have been specifically designed to reduce exposure to these types of radiation, such as EMF shielding

products, and limiting the use of electronic devices whenever possible.

4. For individuals who are looking to track their exposure to toxins, we recommend using a combination of methods, such as personal air monitoring devices, chemical detection kits, and urine testing.

5. For individuals who are interested in taking a more holistic approach to toxin-free living, we recommend incorporating mindfulness practices, such as yoga and meditation, into their daily routine. These practices can help to reduce stress and promote overall health and well-being.

6. Finally, for individuals who are interested in making a larger-scale impact on the environment, we recommend supporting policies and initiatives that promote sustainability and reduce pollution. This may include supporting the use of renewable energy sources, promoting public transportation, and advocating for stricter regulations on industrial pollutants. By working together to create a cleaner, healthier environment, we can all benefit from the many advantages of a toxin-free lifestyle.

Conclusion

Recap of Importance of Avoiding Harmful Substances

In conclusion, it is crucial to understand the importance of avoiding harmful substances in our daily lives. Toxins and other harmful substances can have a significant impact on our health, leading to a range of illnesses and chronic conditions. By taking steps to reduce our exposure to toxins, we can help prevent these negative health outcomes and improve our overall well-being.

Throughout this guide, we have explored a range of methods and tools for tracking and reducing our exposure to toxins, as well as alternative products and services that can help us live a toxin-free life. We have also examined the latest technology and popular brands and devices that can aid us in this process.

By comparing and contrasting these methods, it is clear that there is no one-size-fits-all solution to avoiding harmful substances. The best approach will depend on a range of factors, including personal preferences, budget, and lifestyle.

However, regardless of the specific methods and tools we choose to use, the most important takeaway from this guide is that taking steps to reduce our exposure to toxins is a crucial aspect of maintaining our overall health and well-being. By being aware of the sources of exposure and making conscious choices to reduce our exposure, we can protect ourselves and our loved ones from the harmful effects of toxins and other harmful substances.

In summary, the importance of avoiding harmful substances cannot be overstated. By taking an active role in tracking and reducing our exposure to toxins, we can improve our quality of life and promote a healthier, happier future for ourselves and those around us.

Final Thoughts and Recommendations

In conclusion, it is crucial to take steps to avoid harmful substances in our environment and daily lives. The risks associated with exposure to toxins are numerous and can have serious health consequences, ranging from acute symptoms to chronic diseases. By being mindful of the sources of toxins and employing strategies to reduce exposure, we can help protect ourselves and our loved ones from the harmful effects of these substances.

Throughout this guide, we have explored a range of methods for tracking, reducing, and avoiding exposure to toxins, including the use of technology, alternative products and services, and DIY solutions. Each of these methods has its pros and cons, and it is important to consider them carefully when deciding on the best approach for your needs and budget.

When considering the use of technology, it is essential to research the products and companies thoroughly, as well as to weigh the benefits and potential risks. Some technologies, such as air purifiers and water filtration systems, are well-established and have proven to be effective at reducing exposure to toxins. Other technologies, such as EMF protection devices, are still relatively new and require further study.

Alternative products and services can offer a range of benefits, including reduced exposure to harmful chemicals, support for local businesses, and a smaller environmental footprint. However, it is important to keep in mind that not all alternative products and services are created equal, and it is essential to research the companies and ingredients carefully.

DIY and homemade solutions can be an excellent way to reduce exposure to toxins while also saving money. However, it is crucial to follow safety protocols and ensure that the ingredients and materials used are free from harmful substances.

In general, a combination of methods is likely to be the most effective approach to reducing exposure to toxins. By using a variety of techniques, such as tracking exposure levels, reducing exposure sources, and avoiding harmful substances altogether, we can help safeguard our health and the health of those around us.

In addition to these methods, it is essential to advocate for policies and regulations that prioritize public health and safety. This includes supporting organizations that work to reduce exposure to harmful substances and pushing for legislative changes that promote the use of safer products and practices.

Ultimately, the goal of living a toxin-free life is to promote health, well-being, and longevity. By being mindful of the toxins in our environment and daily lives and taking steps to reduce exposure, we can help protect ourselves and future generations from the harmful effects of these substances.

THE END

Potential References

Introduction

U.S. Department of Health and Human Services. (2019). Report on Carcinogens.

World Health Organization. (2010). Global Burden of Disease: 2004 Update.

World Health Organization. (2016). 10 chemicals of major public health concern.

Chapter 1: Common Toxins and Their Effects

Agency for Toxic Substances and Disease Registry. (2020). Toxicological Profile for Lead.

Centers for Disease Control and Prevention. (2021). Toxic Substances Portal - Mercury.

Environmental Protection Agency. (2021). Basic Information about PFAS.

Chapter 2: Tracking Your Exposure

Environmental Working Group. (n.d.). The Dirty Dozen List of Endocrine Disruptors.

National Institute of Environmental Health Sciences. (2021). How to Reduce Exposure to Environmental Toxins.

Chapter 3: Reducing Your Exposure

Centers for Disease Control and Prevention. (2021). Reduce Your Exposure to Toxic Chemicals at Home.

Environmental Working Group. (n.d.). EWG's Guide to Healthy Cleaning.

Environmental Working Group. (n.d.). Skin Deep Cosmetics Database.

Chapter 4: Toxin-Free Living

Environmental Working Group. (n.d.). EWG's Shopper's Guide to Pesticides in Produce.

National Institute of Environmental Health Sciences. (2021). Non-Toxic Home Cleaning.

Chapter 5: Technology for Toxin-Free Living

Aires Tech. (n.d.). TESLA Gold Series Plug-in.

DefenderShield. (n.d.). DefenderPad Laptop EMF Radiation & Heat Shield.

Chapter 6: Comparing and Contrasting Methods

Consumer Reports. (2019). The Truth About Toxin-Free Products.

Environmental Working Group. (n.d.). EWG's Guide to Healthy Living.

Conclusion

Centers for Disease Control and Prevention. (2021). Reduce Your Risk of Chronic Disease.

Environmental Working Group. (n.d.). The Dirty Dozen List of Endocrine Disruptors.

www.ingramcontent.com/pod-product-compliance
Lightning Source LLC
LaVergne TN
LVHW012127070526
838202LV00056B/5889